About the Author

Hi, my name is Allen M. Card and I am an author of the arts. In my spare time I like to write poetry. I find it amusing. It helps me with my well being. Reading and writing poetry is healthy (I think). My brand is Card's Creative for I am also an artist who makes coloring books. So that's a little bit about me!

About the Book

This is a short but sweet poetry book. It has twenty-four poems in it. The poems are nice and interesting for you to relax and read through. I hope I touched your hearts with this great little poem book. I am Allen Card and I hope you enjoy my poetry.

I just know you will!

Acting

You act the part.

You use your heart.

Acting is also mental, so you use your powers to create a scene. Don't you know what I mean?

Around noon

It was around noon.

Last night I spotted three raccoons.

My sister thinks that I am a loon.

I listened to a tune.

I will eat lunch soon.

And all of this was brought to my attention around noon.

Beauty

My head is nice

When men look at me they think twice.

That is rude and not nice.

Oh! Beauty comes with a great price.

Brothers

A kind heart.

One who is there for you but comes in twos.

Have unconditional love for your brothers even if he does wrong.

You still love him just because he is your brother from the same mother.

Dolphins

A dolphin swims in the pacific ocean. He is a spinner dolphin and he is a beautiful swimmer. They eat fish. Dolphins are the queens of the sea, always traveling the ocean blue. It jumps out of the water and spins. Seeing the dolphins was spectacular. The bottleneck dolphins flip out of the water. They are great too!

Fathers

My father is not strict in his own way.

He lets you make your own decisions and lets you deal with them.

Sin is the main subject, and it is not funny.

Besides, you get more done right without sinning.

I believe this is what fathers are for.

feelings

You feel happy or sad. You can feel bad, sometimes mad.

When you feel sappy then you should take a nappy.

When it is your time to shine you will feel excited and terrified all at the same time.

Fire

Fire is great in the wintertime and even the summer to warm your soul.

You can create a real hot fire using coal.

Some place their fire in a bowl.

When we see fire we say "Oh".

Freedom

Freedom rings in America from shore to shore.

It runs the race, it's America's core.

It screams for more.

You use it when you step out of your front door.

When life gets to be too much of a bore, use your American Freedom.

Illusion

Use your illusion. Your illusion is part of your solution.

Know what your using. Many things are illusions but they are personal in your mind.

Illusions usually happen when your reality is in a bind.

So practice to be kind in your heart and mind.

And that is how you use your illusion.

Item

You usually find your item the last place you check because it is the first place you put it.

Kindness

Many people are kind.

Consider it signed.

Place your life on rewind.

Go out and dine.

Things are fine when your kind.

Learn

We all learn.

Some more than others.

Some burn

You can search knowledge and find a fern.

While you study you can eat corn.

You drive and blow your horn.

All of this can happen as I have learned.

LOVE

A butterfly in the wind.

You love your kin like a mother to a son.

Loving in life isn't a sin.

In love only play to win!

Man

As a man

He went into the night

As an animal

He wants to fight

Here and there

A gentleman's delight

It took time

To keep things right

Now and then

It reached it's height

Too much time

That's enough might

It goes on daily always for tonight. Live for today and tomorrow but keep the present in sight.

Money

It is good to have money so you can buy things for your hunny.

It will make you so happy so that you will be elated like a hopping bunny.

The issue with money isn't too funny.

And it makes you wallet runny.

So, strive to have lots of money.

Nature

The wild does not keep numbers, for it is wild nature. People do but you cannot judge nature. You can't count nature, but you can always rely on it to do its job. We are all interwoven with each other and by the side, under our feet, nature.

Snow

White snow blankets everywhere.

The snow is white while snowflakes fall onto you.

The snow is cold and beautiful.

We play in the snow.

Sometimes you get a lot of snow and at other times just a dusting.

We like it to snow in the winter.

Sunrise

The sun rises. Revealing Everyone's disguises.

It rises on the east coast of America in the morning.

The golden sunrise is adorning.

It is a start of a new day. The sun rises over the bay.

People open their day in their own way.

You can say with the sunrise "It is the start of a new day".

Sunset

I watch the sunset some days. The sun sets at different times of the year but it always happens in the afternoon. I sit on my back porch and watch the sun go down in the west over the pacific ocean. The sky turns orange, red, or pink, and the sun goes down for the day.

The Day

One should look forward to the day.

It is the light of May.

Farmers roll their hay all to make room for the day.

Time

What can't you speed up or slow down and you can't change but stays constant? Time.

Winter FUN

During winter it is cold.

In winter there is ice and snow.

When a blizzard comes we all say "Whoa", and the grass you do not have to mow.

World

The world turns and spins in space.

We humans live on this earth. Everyday we keep up our pace.

Everyday from our birth.

We live with a face. This is what we put fourth.

We can't always have a case.

This is how we show our self-worth.

www.ingramcontent.com/pod-product-compliance
Lightning Source LLC
Chambersburg PA
CBHW071424070526
44578CB00003B/684